The Story of
JOSEPH and His Brothers

By REV. JUDE WINKLER, OFM Conv.

AF207524

Imprimi Potest: Daniel Pietrzak, OFM Conv., Minister Provincial of St. Anthony of Padua Province (USA)
Nihil Obstat: Daniel V. Flynn, J.C.D., Censor Librorum
Imprimatur: Patrick J. Sheridan, Vicar General, Archdiocese of New York

Jacob and his sons

JACOB was one of the Patriarchs, for he was a founding father of the Jewish people. He had a large family which included twelve sons. Of these sons, he loved Joseph the most of all.

Joseph had dreams in which he was more important than his brothers. He dreamt that he was gathering grain and his bundle was higher than that of his brothers.

Joseph is sold by his brothers

JOSEPH's brothers became jealous of him. When he visited them in the fields, they threw him in a pit and planned to kill him.

When they saw some merchants passing by, they decided to sell him to them as a slave for twenty pieces of silver.

3

Jacob is told that Joseph is dead

JACOB had given Joseph a beautiful robe as a sign of his love. To hide what they had done, the brothers dipped Joseph's robe in the blood of a lamb. They showed it to their father, and Jacob believed that Joseph had been killed by wild beasts.

Jacob immediately tore his clothes and threw ashes on his head to mourn for his son. He refused to be comforted for many days.

Joseph becomes Potiphar's slave

THE merchants who had bought Joseph were headed for Egypt. When they arrived there, they sold Joseph as a slave to Potiphar, the chief steward of Pharaoh, the king of Egypt.

God protected Joseph, and Potiphar came to place great confidence in him. Potiphar eventually put Joseph in charge of his entire household.

Joseph refuses to do evil

JOSEPH was honest and pure, but Potiphar's wife was wicked and admired Joseph. She wanted to lead him into sin. One day, when Joseph was alone in the house with her, she tried to pull him into bed.

Joseph refused to break God's law and to betray his master. He ran away from the woman, leaving his cloak in her hands.

Joseph is put in prison

THE wicked woman accused Joseph of betraying his master. Joseph was thrown into prison, but even there God was with him.

The chief keeper of the prison trusted Joseph. He appointed him to look after two of Pharaoh's servants who were also prisoners there. One had been his cupbearer and the other his baker.

Joseph explains dreams

BOTH of these men had dreams which they asked Joseph to interpret. The cupbearer dreamt that he had pressed grapes from three branches and then given the wine to Pharaoh.

Joseph, with God's guidance, told him that God would lift up his head and have him return to Pharaoh's service in three days.

The baker's dream

THE baker dreamt that he was carrying three baskets of bread on his head and the birds were eating the bread in the top basket.

Joseph said that this meant that the baker's head would be lifted off, for he would be put to death in three days.

The dreams are fulfilled

THREE days later, Pharaoh held a great feast for his birthday. He remembered his two servants who were in prison.

He ordered that the cupbearer be released and brought back to his household, just as Joseph had predicted.

10

The baker is put to death

LIKEWISE, Pharaoh gave the order that his baker be put to death for his evil deeds. Once again, Joseph had foreseen what was to happen that day.

The cupbearer had promised Joseph that if he were set free, he would help Joseph. He forgot his promise, though, and Joseph stayed in prison.

Pharaoh's dreams

ONE night, about two years later, Pharaoh had two dreams that greatly troubled him. His wise men could not explain them, so the cup-bearer told him about Joseph and how he had been able to explain his dream.

Pharaoh summoned Joseph from his prison. When Joseph arrived, he told him that he had seen seven fat cows come up from the river and graze in rich marshes. Then seven lean cows came up and ate the fat cows.

The second dream that night

THEN Pharaoh had seen two stalks of wheat with seven heads. One was full, the other was withered. The withered one straightened up and ate the full one.

Pharaoh was frightened because he couldn't understand these dreams and they seemed to foretell evil events.

13

Joseph explains Pharaoh's dreams

JOSEPH told Pharaoh that the dreams meant that there would be seven years of plenty followed by seven years of famine.

He advised Pharaoh to store up grain during the seven years of plenty, so that there would be food when the famine came.

Joseph is made Pharaoh's assistant

PHARAOH was greatly impressed with the wisdom of Joseph. He placed him over all his work, and over all the affairs of the kingdom.

As a sign of Joseph's authority, Pharaoh put his own ring on Joseph's hand, dressed him in linen, and put a gold chain around his neck. He ordered that all should pay him honor when he rode by on his chariot.

So Joseph stored up huge quantities of grain to prepare for the lean years.

The years of plenty

IN this way, the years of plenty began. The annual floods of the Nile were generous and brought great fertility to the land. The grain harvests were greater than they had ever been before.

All during this period, Joseph bought grain from the people. He built many buildings to store it for the famine which was coming.

This lasted for seven years, as Joseph had said.

The years of famine

WHEN the seven years ended, the famine came—just as Joseph had foretold. The Nile did not flood at all, which meant that the farmers could not plant their crops. The drought became very severe and spread over the whole earth.

During this bitter time, both people and animals did not have food. Many of them were in danger of death because of hunger and thirst.

Joseph feeds the Egyptians

I N Egypt, though, there was no hunger because
God had blessed the people in Joseph.

The grain had been stored up year after year, and the grain bins were now filled.

Joseph threw open the grain bins and sold all of this grain to all of the people in need.

Joseph feeds the surrounding peoples

THE harvests in all of the Nile valley failed for seven years in a row, but grain had been stored up.

When the Egyptian carts filled with food arrived in the different regions, there was feasting and rejoicing. All the starving people were told, "Go to Joseph!" He saved all of them from starvation.

Joseph's brothers come seeking food

CANAAN, the land of Jacob and his sons, also suffered from the famine. Jacob sent his sons to Egypt to buy grain. Only Benjamin, the youngest, remained at home, for Jacob was afraid that something would happen to him as it had happened to Joseph.

When Joseph's brothers came before him, Joseph knew them at once. They didn't recognize him, because he was dressed like an Egyptian. He didn't tell them who he was, for he wanted to test them.

Joseph treats his brothers harshly

A T first Joseph accused his brothers of being spies. He told them that he would hold one of them in prison until they returned with their youngest brother, Benjamin.

He also had the money that they had used to pay for the grain put back into their sacks of grain.

Joseph's brothers find their money restored

THE brothers returned to their father. Only then did they discover that their money had been returned—hidden in the bags of grain. They were frightened because they thought that Joseph would accuse them of stealing the money.

Jacob did not want Benjamin to go to Egypt, but the famine grew worse and so he sent him with his brothers when they went for more grain.

Joseph gives a banquet for his brothers

ON their second visit to Egypt, Joseph gave a rich banquet for his brothers. They were served rich food and good wine.

Joseph gave Benjamin five times as much food as any of the others received, but the brothers did not yet know why because they still didn't recognize Joseph.

23

Joseph is moved to tears

JOSEPH was so moved by seeing Benjamin that he had to leave the banquet hall and he wept.

Then he washed his face and went back into the banquet to feast with his brothers.

Joseph again tests his brothers

JOSEPH told one of his servants to put an expensive silver cup in Benjamin's sack. They searched the sacks and found it. Joseph said that since Benjamin had stolen it, Benjamin had to become his slave.

On hearing this, Judah, Joseph's brother, offered to become a slave in Benjamin's place. When Joseph heard this, he could no longer hide his feelings.

25

Joseph makes himself known
to his brothers

JOSEPH realized that his brothers were no longer filled with jealousy but were willing to love each other just the way they were. He cried out to them: "I am Joseph!"

At first, the brothers were afraid of Joseph, but he came down from his throne and embraced his brothers. There was such great rejoicing that even the neighbors heard them celebrate. Pharaoh invited Joseph's entire family to come and settle in Egypt.

Jacob and his whole family move to Egypt

JOSEPH sent a caravan to bring his father and all of their goods down to Egypt to be with him. At first Jacob didn't want to go, but God told him that this was His will.

So he set out on the long journey with his sons, their wives, and their children. There were about seventy people in all.

The family settles in Goshen

THE family traveled until they reached the land of Egypt. Because Joseph was such an important person in the land and Pharaoh loved him greatly, he honored his family and let them settle in the land of Goshen.

Pharaoh gave them the best fields in all of Goshen and even put them in charge of his own cattle.

Joseph is reunited with his father

AS soon as he saw his father, Joseph embraced him and wept tears of joy. Jacob's heart was also glad to see his beloved son once again.

The whole family, united once again, thanked God for His mercy and kindness to them.

Jacob blesses his sons

BEFORE he died, Jacob called each of his sons to his bed and he gave each of them a share in the great promise of God.

He also adopted Joseph's two sons, Ephraim and Manasseh, and gave them each a full share in his inheritance.

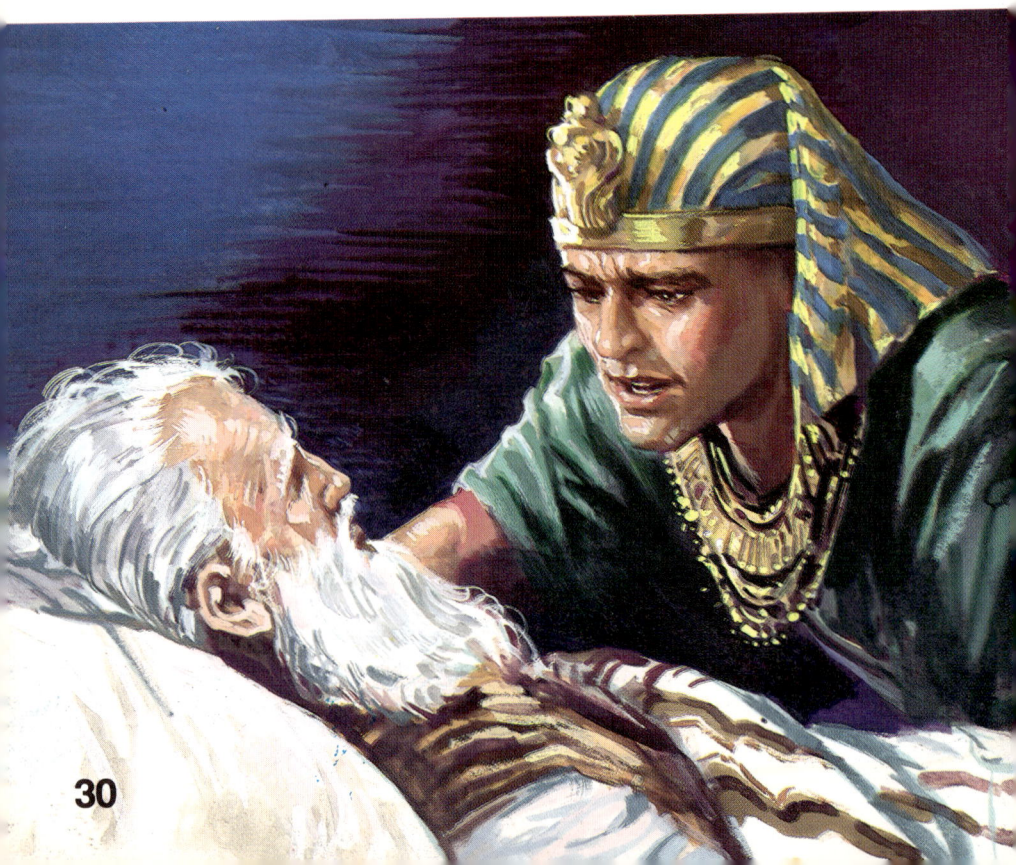

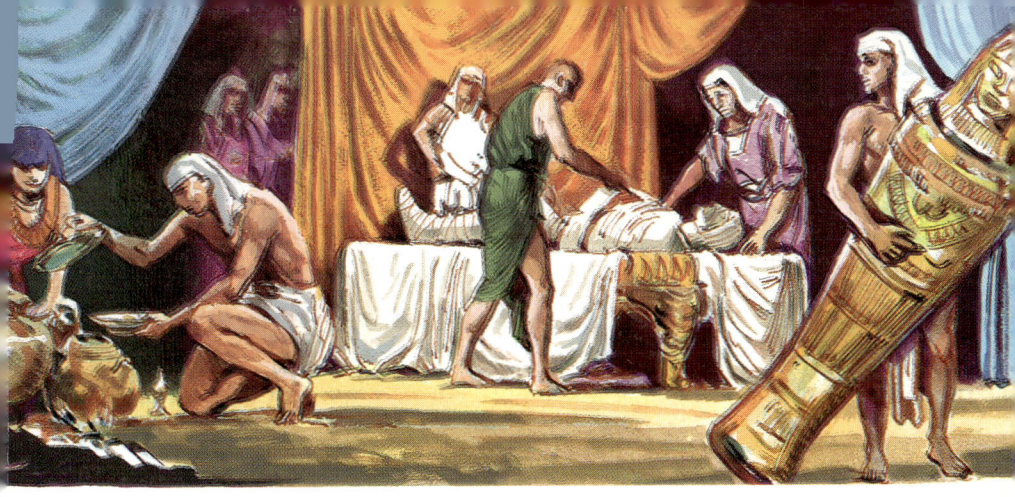

Joseph buries his father and remains in Egypt

WHEN Jacob died, Joseph had his body prepared and he ordered that all of Egypt mourn for seventy days. Joseph and his brothers then took his body to Canaan where they buried him.

Afterward, Joseph returned to Egypt and lived out his life in peace. Before he died, he told his brothers that God had willed that they all come to Egypt in order to save them from the famine.

He also told them that God would one day take them out of Egypt to return to the land that had been promised to Abraham, Isaac, and Jacob.

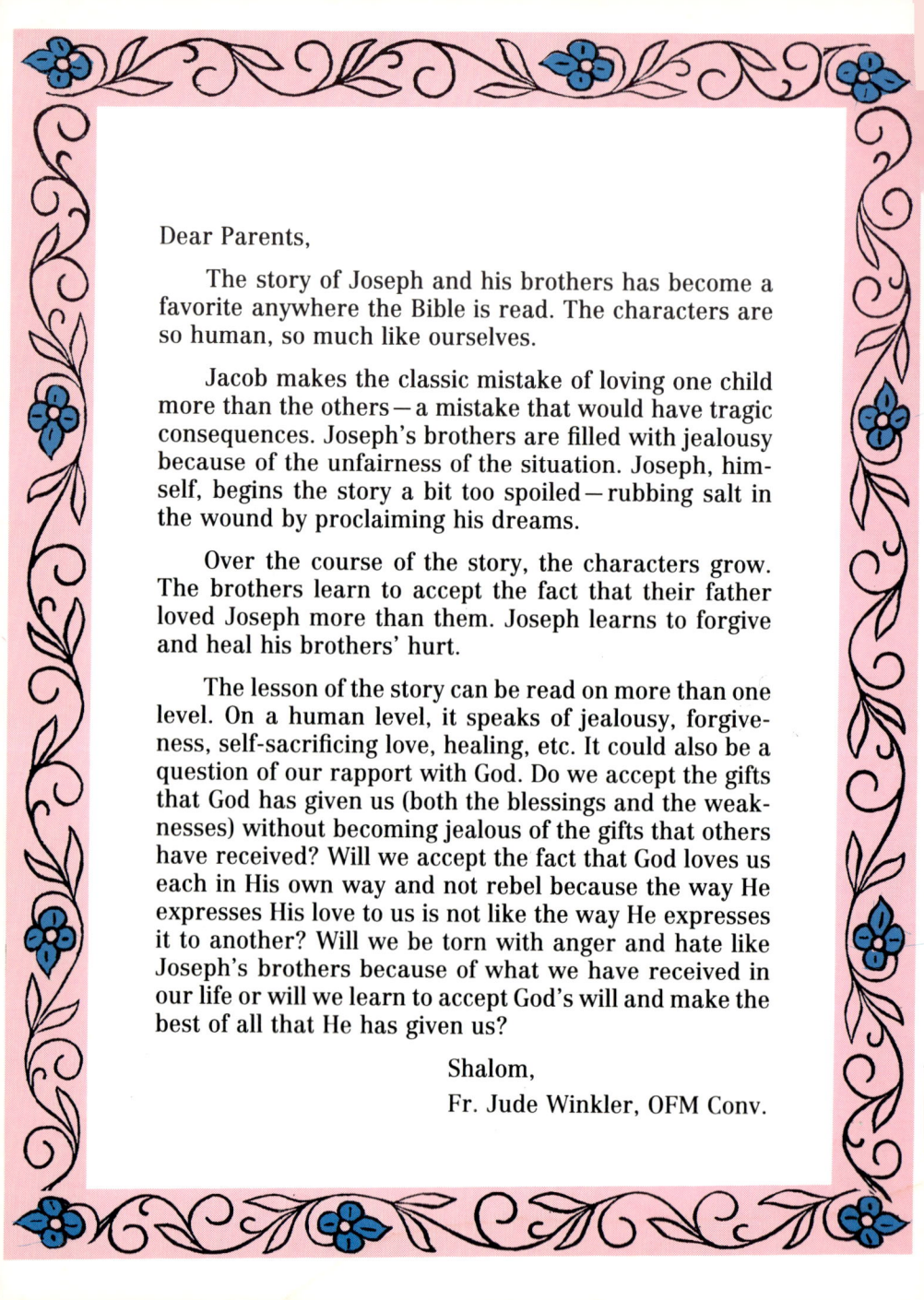

Dear Parents,

The story of Joseph and his brothers has become a favorite anywhere the Bible is read. The characters are so human, so much like ourselves.

Jacob makes the classic mistake of loving one child more than the others — a mistake that would have tragic consequences. Joseph's brothers are filled with jealousy because of the unfairness of the situation. Joseph, himself, begins the story a bit too spoiled — rubbing salt in the wound by proclaiming his dreams.

Over the course of the story, the characters grow. The brothers learn to accept the fact that their father loved Joseph more than them. Joseph learns to forgive and heal his brothers' hurt.

The lesson of the story can be read on more than one level. On a human level, it speaks of jealousy, forgiveness, self-sacrificing love, healing, etc. It could also be a question of our rapport with God. Do we accept the gifts that God has given us (both the blessings and the weaknesses) without becoming jealous of the gifts that others have received? Will we accept the fact that God loves us each in His own way and not rebel because the way He expresses His love to us is not like the way He expresses it to another? Will we be torn with anger and hate like Joseph's brothers because of what we have received in our life or will we learn to accept God's will and make the best of all that He has given us?

Shalom,
Fr. Jude Winkler, OFM Conv.